Redwood Reg
Flower Finder

Guide to Identifying Wildflowers of
the Coastal Fog Belt of California

Second Edition

by Phoebe Watts
illustrated by Sarah Ellen Watts

Identifies wildflowers growing in the range
of the Redwood tree, *Sequoia sempervirens*.

Nature Study Guild Publishers • Rochester, New York • www.naturestudy.com

terms that describe flowers

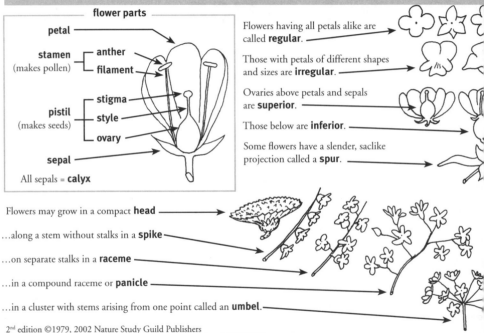

flower parts

petal

stamen (makes pollen) — **anther**, **filament**

pistil (makes seeds) — **stigma**, **style**, **ovary**

sepal

All sepals = **calyx**

Flowers having all petals alike are called **regular**.

Those with petals of different shapes and sizes are **irregular**.

Ovaries above petals and sepals are **superior**.

Those below are **inferior**.

Some flowers have a slender, saclike projection called a **spur**.

Flowers may grow in a compact **head**

…along a stem without stalks in a **spike**

…on separate stalks in a **raceme**

…in a compound raceme or **panicle**

…in a cluster with stems arising from one point called an **umbel**.

2nd edition ©1979, 2002 Nature Study Guild Publishers
ISBN 0-912550-25-2 Library of Congress Control Number: 2001098790

terms that describe plants

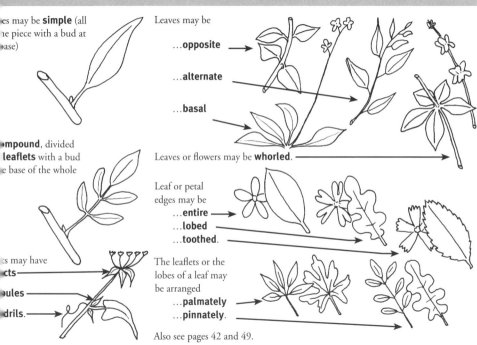

...es may be **simple** (all ...ne piece with a bud at ...ase)

...mpound, divided ... **leaflets** with a bud ...e base of the whole

...s may have

...cts

...ules

...drils.

Leaves may be

...**opposite**

...**alternate**

...**basal**

Leaves or flowers may be **whorled**.

Leaf or petal edges may be
...**entire**
...**lobed**
...**toothed**.

The leaflets or the lobes of a leaf may be arranged
...**palmately**
...**pinnately**.

Also see pages 42 and 49.

to use this book

Begin on the next page with the first choice: either or and follow directions.

about this book

Habitat symbols show the kinds of places within the redwood region where you're most likely to find each flower.

 shady forest

 edge of forest

 open places

 wet places

Trees and shrubs, and plants growing on sea bluffs and beaches, are not included in this book.

The months when a plant usually blooms are printed next to its picture.

jun-aug

You may want to use a hand lens to see some features used for identification in this key.

---

about plant names

Common names are printed like this:
Fireweed

The Latin name is printed like this:
Epilobium angustifolium

The first part of the Latin, or scientific, name is the genus (plural: genera). The second part is the species—the kind of plant within the genus. Related genera are grouped in families. Some common characteristics, and the Latin family name, are given for plant families with more than one species in this book. Families with only one species in this book are named underneath the Latin name for that plant.

Names of plants in this edition conform to those in *The Jepson Manual: Higher Plants of California*, James C. Hickman, ed., University of California Press, Berkeley, 1993.

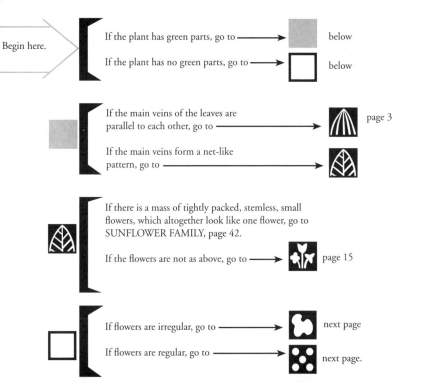

Begin here.

If the plant has green parts, go to → below

If the plant has no green parts, go to → below

If the main veins of the leaves are parallel to each other, go to → page 3

If the main veins form a net-like pattern, go to →

If there is a mass of tightly packed, stemless, small flowers, which altogether look like one flower, go to SUNFLOWER FAMILY, page 42.

If the flowers are not as above, go to → page 15

If flowers are irregular, go to → next page

If flowers are regular, go to → next page.

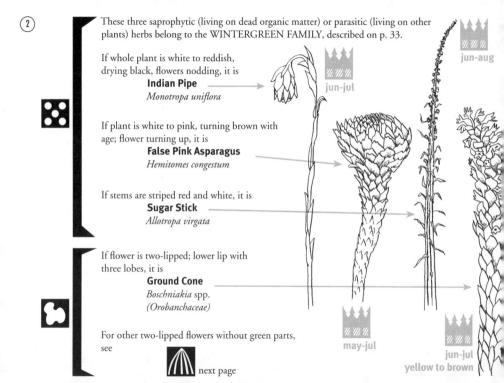

(2)

These three saprophytic (living on dead organic matter) or parasitic (living on other plants) herbs belong to the WINTERGREEN FAMILY, described on p. 33.

If whole plant is white to reddish, drying black, flowers nodding, it is
Indian Pipe
Monotropa uniflora

jun-jul

jun-aug

If plant is white to pink, turning brown with age; flower turning up, it is
False Pink Asparagus
Hemitomes congestum

If stems are striped red and white, it is
Sugar Stick
Allotropa virgata

If flower is two-lipped; lower lip with three lobes, it is
Ground Cone
Boschniakia spp.
(Orobanchaceae)

For other two-lipped flowers without green parts, see

next page

may-jul

jun-jul
yellow to brown

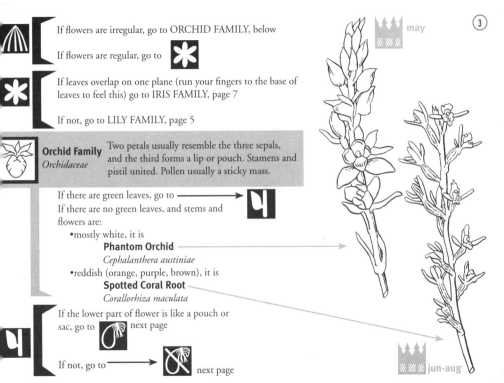

If flowers are irregular, go to ORCHID FAMILY, below

If flowers are regular, go to

If leaves overlap on one plane (run your fingers to the base of leaves to feel this) go to IRIS FAMILY, page 7

If not, go to LILY FAMILY, page 5

Orchid Family
Orchidaceae
Two petals usually resemble the three sepals, and the third forms a lip or pouch. Stamens and pistil united. Pollen usually a sticky mass.

If there are green leaves, go to
If there are no green leaves, and stems and flowers are:
• mostly white, it is
Phantom Orchid
Cephalanthera austiniae
• reddish (orange, purple, brown), it is
Spotted Coral Root
Corallorhiza maculata

If the lower part of flower is like a pouch or sac, go to next page

If not, go to next page

may

jun-aug

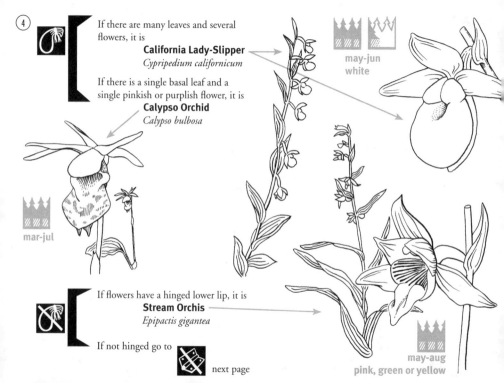

(4)

If there are many leaves and several flowers, it is
California Lady-Slipper
Cypripedium californicum

may-jun
white

If there is a single basal leaf and a single pinkish or purplish flower, it is
Calypso Orchid
Calypso bulbosa

mar-jul

If flowers have a hinged lower lip, it is
Stream Orchis
Epipactis gigantea

If not hinged go to next page

may-aug
pink, green or yellow

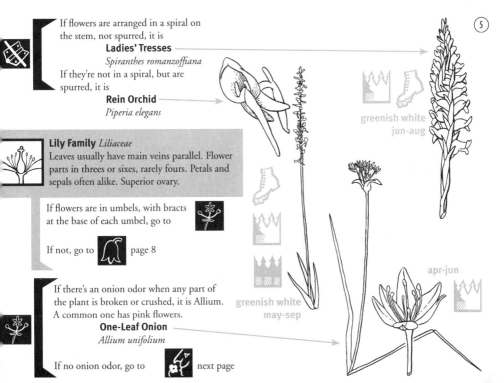

If flowers are arranged in a spiral on the stem, not spurred, it is

Ladies' Tresses
Spiranthes romanzoffiana

If they're not in a spiral, but are spurred, it is

Rein Orchid
Piperia elegans

greenish white
jun-aug

Lily Family *Liliaceae*
Leaves usually have main veins parallel. Flower parts in threes or sixes, rarely fours. Petals and sepals often alike. Superior ovary.

If flowers are in umbels, with bracts at the base of each umbel, go to

If not, go to page 8

If there's an onion odor when any part of the plant is broken or crushed, it is Allium. A common one has pink flowers.

One-Leaf Onion
Allium unifolium

If no onion odor, go to next page

greenish white
may-sep

apr-jun

If flowers are red, hanging, with tiny green petals turning back at the ends, it is
Firecracker Flower →
Dichelostemma ida-maia

If they're blue-purple, not hanging, go to

If flowers are on long stalks, it is
Ithuriel's Spear, Grass Nut →
Triteleia laxa

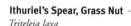

If they're tightly clustered, almost in heads, go to

If flowers have six stamens and are in true umbels (all the flower stems arise from same point) it is **mar-may**
Blue Dicks, Wild Hyacinth
Dichelostemma capitatum

If flowers have three stamens, and close examination of the tight cluster shows that all flower stems do not start at exactly the same point, it is
Ookow →
Dichelostemma congestum

apr-jun

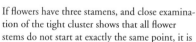

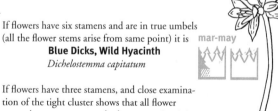

may-jul

apr-

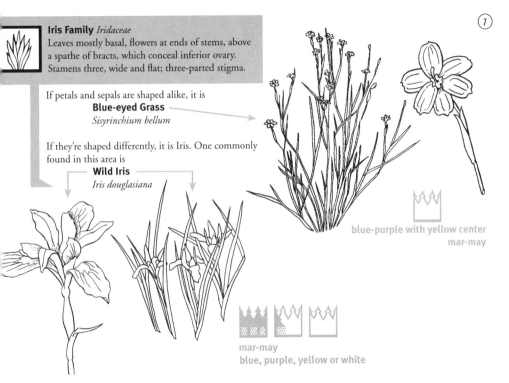

Iris Family *Iridaceae*
Leaves mostly basal, flowers at ends of stems, above a spathe of bracts, which conceal inferior ovary. Stamens three, wide and flat; three-parted stigma.

If petals and sepals are shaped alike, it is
Blue-eyed Grass
Sisyrinchium bellum

If they're shaped differently, it is Iris. One commonly found in this area is
Wild Iris
Iris douglasiana

blue-purple with yellow center
mar-may

mar-may
blue, purple, yellow or white

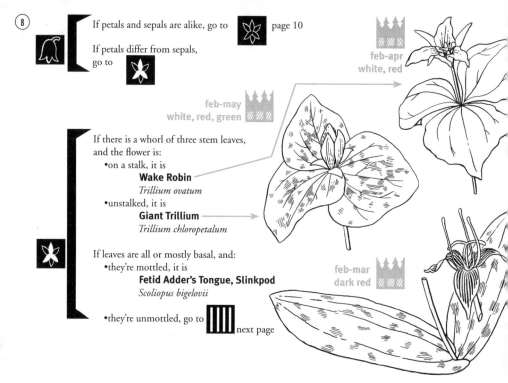

If petals and sepals are alike, go to page 10

If petals differ from sepals, go to

feb-may
white, red, green

feb-apr
white, red

If there is a whorl of three stem leaves, and the flower is:
- on a stalk, it is
  Wake Robin
  Trillium ovatum
- unstalked, it is
  Giant Trillium
  Trillium chloropetalum

If leaves are all or mostly basal, and:
- they're mottled, it is
  Fetid Adder's Tongue, Slinkpod
  Scoliopus bigelovii

- they're unmottled, go to next page

feb-mar
dark red

If flowers are hanging, it is
Fairy Lanterns, Golden Globe Tulip ───→
Calochortus amabilis

apr-jun
yellow

If they face up, go to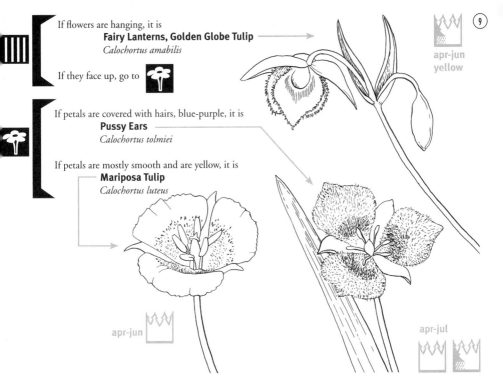

If petals are covered with hairs, blue-purple, it is
Pussy Ears
Calochortus tolmiei

If petals are mostly smooth and are yellow, it is
Mariposa Tulip
Calochortus luteus

apr-jun

apr-jul

If leaves grow on stems, go to **page 12**

If leaves are basal, or attached very near the ground, go to

If flowers are dark: red, blue or purple, go to **next page**

If they're pale: white, cream, pale pink, and:

• leaves are light-mottled; flower white to cream with a yellow stripe, it is
Fawn Lily
Erythronium californicum
(Flower pink, it's *E. revolutum* or *E. oregonum*)

• leaves have wavy margins; flower open only early morning and late day, it is
Soap Plant
Chlorogalum pomeridianum

• leaves are narrow, grasslike, with dry, splitting edges, it is
Bear Grass
Xerophyllum tenax

• leaves have smooth edges, it is
Star Lily
Zigadenus fremontii

apr-may

may-jul
white

next page

If the leaves are:
- ovate, shiny, and the flowers are pink to magenta, it is
  Bead Lily
  Clintonia andrewsiana

- lanceolate, flowers blue-purple, it is **Camas**
  Camassia quamash

- oblong, dull; flowers red, it is
  Coast Lily
  Lilium maritimum

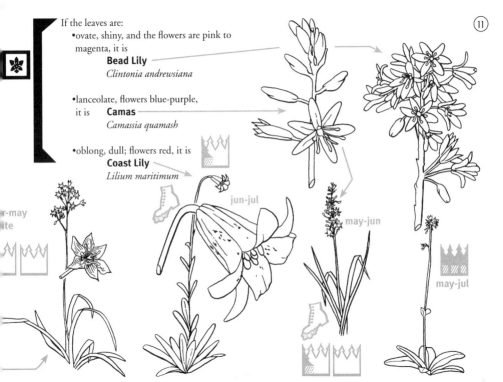

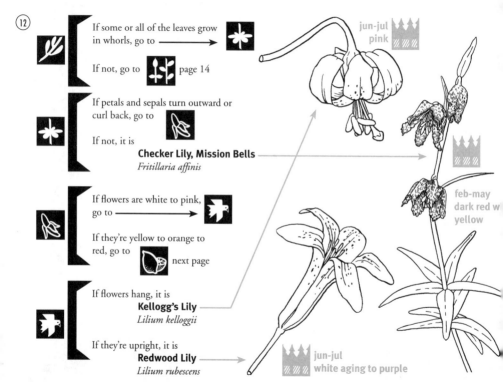

If some or all of the leaves grow in whorls, go to ➝

If not, go to page 14

If petals and sepals turn outward or curl back, go to

If not, it is
Checker Lily, Mission Bells
Fritillaria affinis

If flowers are white to pink, go to ➝

If they're yellow to orange to red, go to next page

If flowers hang, it is
Kellogg's Lily
Lilium kelloggii

If they're upright, it is
Redwood Lily
Lilium rubescens

jun-jul
pink

feb-may
dark red w
yellow

jun-jul
white aging to purple

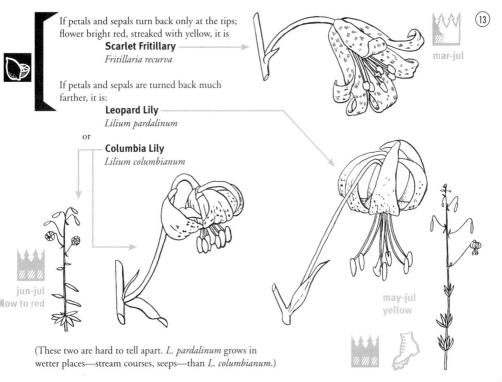

If petals and sepals turn back only at the tips;
flower bright red, streaked with yellow, it is
Scarlet Fritillary
Fritillaria recurva

mar-jul

If petals and sepals are turned back much
farther, it is:
Leopard Lily
Lilium pardalinum

or

Columbia Lily
Lilium columbianum

jun-jul
low to red

may-jul
yellow

(These two are hard to tell apart. *L. pardalinum* grows in
wetter places—stream courses, seeps—than *L. columbianum*.)

(13)

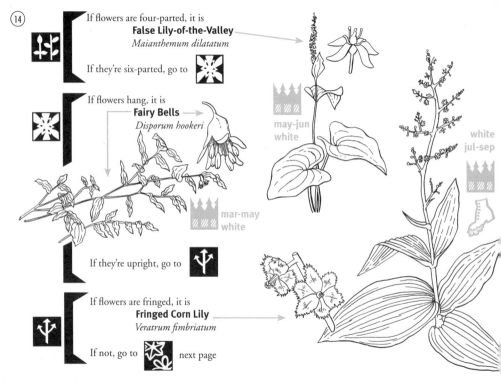

(14)

If flowers are four-parted, it is
False Lily-of-the-Valley
Maianthemum dilatatum

If they're six-parted, go to

If flowers hang, it is
Fairy Bells
Disporum hookeri

If they're upright, go to

mar-may
white

may-jun
white

white
jul-sep

If flowers are fringed, it is
Fringed Corn Lily
Veratrum fimbriatum

If not, go to ⭐ next page

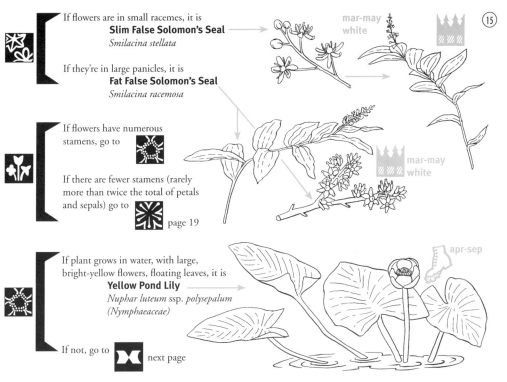

If flowers are in small racemes, it is
Slim False Solomon's Seal
Smilacina stellata

mar-may
white

If they're in large panicles, it is
Fat False Solomon's Seal
Smilacina racemosa

If flowers have numerous
stamens, go to

If there are fewer stamens (rarely
more than twice the total of petals
and sepals) go to

page 19

mar-may
white

If plant grows in water, with large,
bright-yellow flowers, floating leaves, it is
Yellow Pond Lily
Nuphar luteum ssp. *polysepalum*
(Nymphaeaceae)

apr-sep

If not, go to

next page

If stamens are united by their filaments into a sheath around the pistil, the whole forming a club-like center, it is

If stamens are separate, go to

(Fruit is like little wheel)

Mallow, Cheeses
Malva neglecta
(Malvaceae)

may-oct
lilac, white

If sepals are united at their bases to form a calyx tube to which petals and stamens are attached, go to ROSE FAMILY.

If sepals, petals and stamens are all separate, go to next page

mar-jun

Rose Family *Rosaceae*
Leaves usually alternate, with stipules. Flowers regular. Sepals and petals at edge of a flower tube which is lined with a glandular disc.

If leaves are three parted; flowers white, it is
Woodland Strawberry ⟶
Fragaria vesca

If leaves are five to nine-parted; flowers creamy to white-yellow, it is
Sticky Potentilla ⟶
Potentilla glandulosa

may-

If there is one pistil, go to 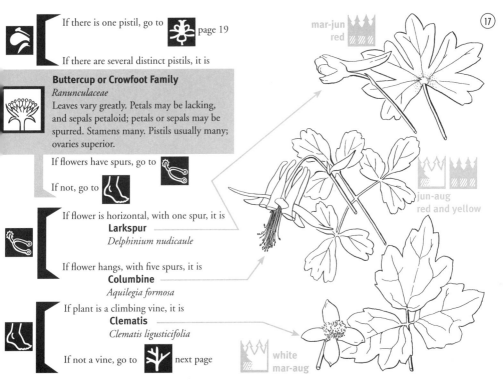 page 19

If there are several distinct pistils, it is

Buttercup or Crowfoot Family
Ranunculaceae
Leaves vary greatly. Petals may be lacking, and sepals petaloid; petals or sepals may be spurred. Stamens many. Pistils usually many; ovaries superior.

If flowers have spurs, go to

If not, go to

If flower is horizontal, with one spur, it is
Larkspur
Delphinium nudicaule

If flower hangs, with five spurs, it is
Columbine
Aquilegia formosa

If plant is a climbing vine, it is
Clematis
Clematis ligusticifolia

If not a vine, go to next page

mar-jun
red

jun-aug
red and yellow

white
mar-aug

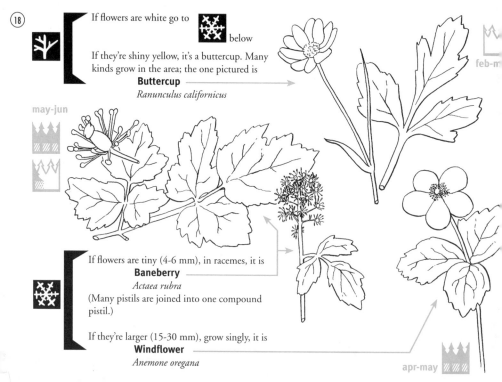

(18)

If flowers are white go to ✳ below

If they're shiny yellow, it's a buttercup. Many kinds grow in the area; the one pictured is
Buttercup
Ranunculus californicus

feb-m

may-jun

If flowers are tiny (4-6 mm), in racemes, it is
Baneberry
Actaea rubra
(Many pistils are joined into one compound pistil.)

If they're larger (15-30 mm), grow singly, it is
Windflower
Anemone oregana

apr-may

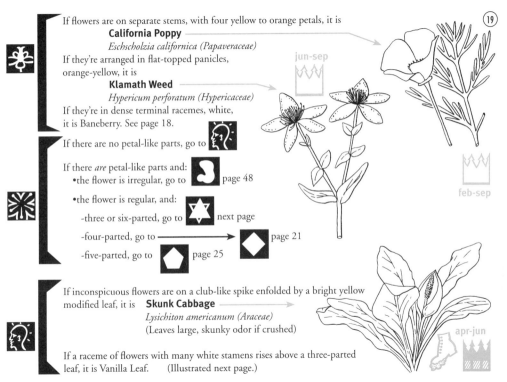

If flowers are on separate stems, with four yellow to orange petals, it is
California Poppy
Eschscholzia californica (Papaveraceae)

If they're arranged in flat-topped panicles, orange-yellow, it is
Klamath Weed
Hypericum perforatum (Hypericaceae)

If they're in dense terminal racemes, white, it is Baneberry. See page 18.

If there are no petal-like parts, go to

If there *are* petal-like parts and:
- the flower is irregular, go to page 48
- the flower is regular, and:
  - three or six-parted, go to next page
  - four-parted, go to page 21
  - five-parted, go to page 25

If inconspicuous flowers are on a club-like spike enfolded by a bright yellow modified leaf, it is **Skunk Cabbage**
Lysichiton americanum (Araceae)
(Leaves large, skunky odor if crushed)

If a raceme of flowers with many white stamens rises above a three-parted leaf, it is Vanilla Leaf. (Illustrated next page.)

jun-sep

feb-sep

apr-jun

If flowers are above a whorl of
leaves at the top of the stem, and:
- •flowers have three petals, go to page 8
- •flowers have six petals,
  go to PRIMROSE FAMILY, page 41.

If six petals sweep strongly backward,
go to BARBERRY FAMILY.

If there are three petal-like maroon-
colored sepals, go to BIRTHWORT
FAMILY, next page.

Barberry Family *Berberidaceae*
Leaves (in the species below)
compound. Flowers regular.

If leaves are basal; leaflets barely three-lobed,
glossy; flowers 6-8 mm long, it is
Redwood Ivy, Inside-Out Flower
Vancouveria planipetala
(Leaves not glossy, flowers 10-14 mm, it is
Vancouveria hexandra, not illus.)

If leaves are large, three-parted; spikes of petal-less flowers with
white stamens rising above them, it is
Vanilla Leaf
Achlys triphylla

white to lavender
may-jun

white
apr-jun

Birthwort Family *Aristolochiaceae*
No petals. Colored parts are sepals.
Pollinated by flies that are attracted by
the color and carrion scent.

If leaves are basal, smell of ginger when
crushed, it is
> **Wild Ginger** ──────
> *Asarum caudatum*

If the plant is a vine, it is
> **Pipevine**
> *Aristolochia californica*

If the petals are thread-like, dark red,
go to SAXIFRAGE FAMILY, page 30.

If the petals are white, leaves heart-
shaped with main veins parallel,
go to page 14

If the petals are lavender to magenta, swept
back, go to PRIMROSE FAMILY, page 41.

If petals are blue, go to Speedwell, p. 55, or
Synthyris, p. 57.

If none of the above apply, go to ◆ next page

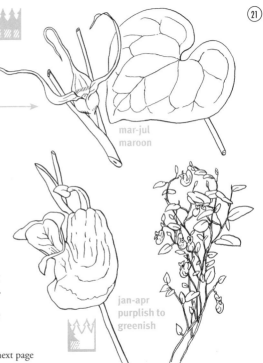

mar-jul
maroon

jan-apr
purplish to
greenish

(21)

(22)

If flowers are tightly clustered, surrounded by four showy, petal-like bracts, it is **Bunchberry**

Cornus canadensis
(Cornaceae)

If flowers have eight stamens, inferior ovary, go to EVENING PRIMROSE FAMILY, page 24.

If they have six stamens, superior ovary, it is

Mustard Family *Brassicaceae*
Juice pungent. Flowers have four petals (narrowed at bases). Four sepals. Six stamens (four long and two short).

If flowers are bright yellow or orange, go to

If they're white, pale yellow or purple, go to next page

If leaves clasp the stem, and are often divided or compound, it is **Field Mustard**
Brassica rapa
If leaves are not clasping, are simple, it is
Wallflower
Erysimum capitatum

may-jul
white

jan-sep
lemon yellow

mar-
golden yello

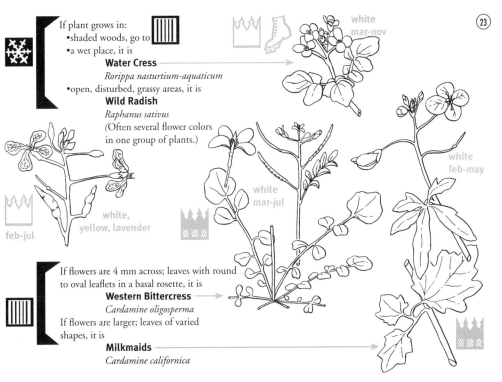

If plant grows in:
- •shaded woods, go to
- •a wet place, it is

Water Cress
Rorippa nasturtium-aquaticum

- •open, disturbed, grassy areas, it is

Wild Radish
Raphanus sativus
(Often several flower colors
in one group of plants.)

white
mar-nov

white
mar-jul

white
feb-may

white,
yellow, lavender

feb-jul

If flowers are 4 mm across; leaves with round
to oval leaflets in a basal rosette, it is
Western Bittercress
Cardamine oligosperma
If flowers are larger; leaves of varied
shapes, it is

Milkmaids
Cardamine californica

Evening Primrose Family *Onagraceae*
Simple leaves. Flower parts in fours. Petals
and sepals are attached above an inferior
ovary, which is often slender, stem-like.

If flower is slender, tubular, with scarlet sepals and
petals; plant forming mats, it is
> **California Fuchsia** (illus. next page)
> *Epilobium septentrionale*

If petals each are divided into three lobes, bright
pink, (may be striped or streaked), it is
> **Red Ribbons**
> *Clarkia concinna*

If petals are not lobed, and there are:
• four sepals, petals lilac-purple to rose
(occasionally white) it is
> **Fireweed**
> *Epilobium angustifolium*
> (A smaller plant, leaves opposite,
> is *Epilobium watsonii*.)

• two sepals pushed to one side, petals pink,
blotched with red, it is
> **Farewell to Spring**
> *Clarkia amoena*

may-jul

jun-au

jul-sep

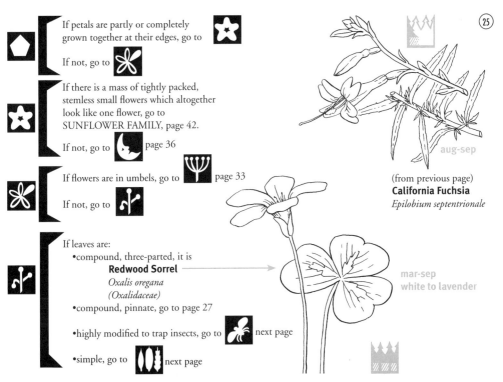

If petals are partly or completely grown together at their edges, go to

If not, go to

If there is a mass of tightly packed, stemless small flowers which altogether look like one flower, go to SUNFLOWER FAMILY, page 42.

If not, go to page 36

If flowers are in umbels, go to page 33

If not, go to

(from previous page)
California Fuchsia
Epilobium septentrionale

aug-sep

If leaves are:
- compound, three-parted, it is
  Redwood Sorrel
  Oxalis oregana
  (Oxalidaceae)
- compound, pinnate, go to page 27

- highly modified to trap insects, go to next page

- simple, go to next page

mar-sep
white to lavender

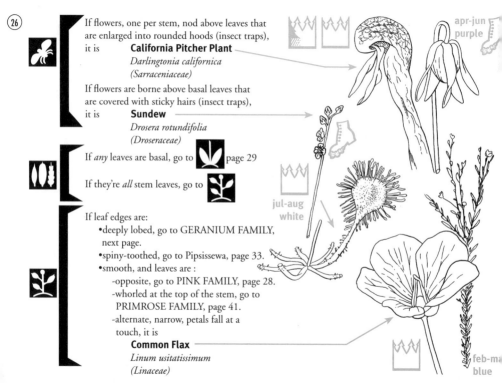

If flowers, one per stem, nod above leaves that
are enlarged into rounded hoods (insect traps),
it is **California Pitcher Plant**
Darlingtonia californica
(Sarraceniaceae)

apr-jun
purple

If flowers are borne above basal leaves that
are covered with sticky hairs (insect traps),
it is **Sundew**
Drosera rotundifolia
(Droseraceae)

If *any* leaves are basal, go to page 29

If they're *all* stem leaves, go to

jul-aug
white

If leaf edges are:
  •deeply lobed, go to GERANIUM FAMILY,
    next page.
  •spiny-toothed, go to Pipsissewa, page 33.
  •smooth, and leaves are :
    -opposite, go to PINK FAMILY, page 28.
    -whorled at the top of the stem, go to
      PRIMROSE FAMILY, page 41.
    -alternate, narrow, petals fall at a
      touch, it is
        Common Flax
        Linum usitatissimum
        (Linaceae)

feb-ma
blue

apr-jul

Geranium Family *Geraniaceae*
Ten stamens. Five styles, which form a pointed column in the center of the flower, and coil up when dry. These two have pink or red flowers.

If leaves are deeply palmately lobed, it is
Wild Geranium, Cranesbill
Geranium carolinianum

If they're pinnately compound, it is
Storksbill, Filaree
Erodium moschatum

(If they're doubly pinnately compound, fernlike, it is *E. cicutarium*, not illus.)

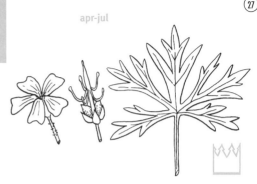

feb-may

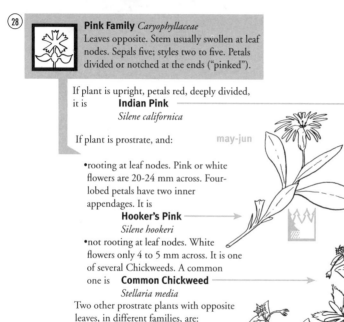

(28)

Pink Family *Caryophyllaceae*
Leaves opposite. Stem usually swollen at leaf nodes. Sepals five; styles two to five. Petals divided or notched at the ends ("pinked").

If plant is upright, petals red, deeply divided, it is **Indian Pink**
Silene californica

mar-aug

If plant is prostrate, and:

may-jun

•rooting at leaf nodes. Pink or white flowers are 20-24 mm across. Four-lobed petals have two inner appendages. It is
Hooker's Pink
Silene hookeri

•not rooting at leaf nodes. White flowers only 4 to 5 mm across. It is one of several Chickweeds. A common one is **Common Chickweed**
Stellaria media

Two other prostrate plants with opposite leaves, in different families, are:
•Orange flowers 4-5 mm across, go to PRIMROSE FAMILY, page 41.
•Small white flowers in terminal clusters, go to SAXIFRAGE FAMILY, page 30.

feb-sep

If leaf edges have lobes or teeth, go to
SAXIFRAGE FAMILY, next page.
If leaf edges are smooth and:
• leaves leathery, mottled white, go to Wild Wintergreen, page 33.
• leaves not leathery:
 • flowers hanging with petals turned back,
  go to PRIMROSE FAMILY, page 41.
 • flowers not so, it is

feb-may
white to pinkish

Portulaca or Purslane Family
Portulacaceae
Leaves fleshy but not thick. Stamens usually
five, opposite petals. Two sepals.

If tiny flowers arise above a disc-like leaf that sur-
rounds the stem, it is
Miner's Lettuce
Claytonia perfoliata
If stem leaves are opposite, it is
Siberian Candyflower
Claytonia sibirica
If stem leaves are alternate, it is
Narrow-leaved Miner's Lettuce
Claytonia parvifolia (not illus.)

If basal leaves have tiny teeth, and there are no
stem leaves at all, go to California Saxifrage, next
page.

mar-sep
all white, or white with pink lines

Saxifrage Family *Saxifragaceae*
Stamens five or ten. Usually two hornlike
styles. These plants are often found on
stream banks or moist, rocky ledges.

may-jun

If flower has *four* thread-like, dark red petals,
it is **Piggyback plant**
Tolmiea menziesii

If petals are five, with:
• flowers in terminal clusters on a
prostrate plant, leaves opposite, it is
Yerba de Selva
Whipplea modesta

white
apr-jun

 next page

• flowers in a raceme, go to ➙ next page

• flowers in a panicle, go to

If there are small basal leaves with teeth but not lobes,
no stem leaves, it is
California Saxifrage
Saxifraga californica

If there are many stem leaves and a tuft of basal leaves
with three to five lobes, branching flower stalks, it is
Boykinia
Boykinia occidentalis   illus. next page

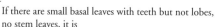

white
feb-jun

If petals are divided, go to 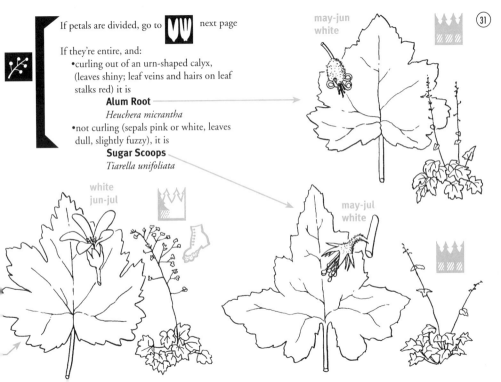 next page

If they're entire, and:
- curling out of an urn-shaped calyx, (leaves shiny; leaf veins and hairs on leaf stalks red) it is
  Alum Root
  Heuchera micrantha
- not curling (sepals pink or white, leaves dull, slightly fuzzy), it is
  Sugar Scoops
  Tiarella unifoliata

may-jun white

white jun-jul

may-jul white

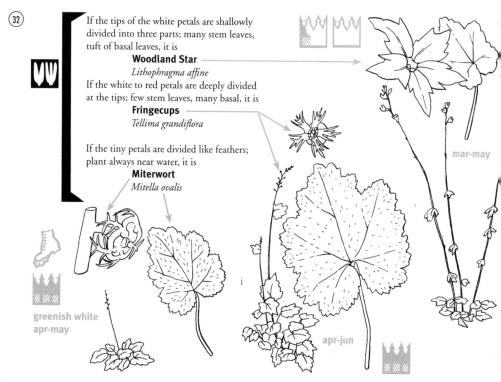

If the tips of the white petals are shallowly divided into three parts; many stem leaves, tuft of basal leaves, it is
Woodland Star
Lithophragma affine

If the white to red petals are deeply divided at the tips; few stem leaves, many basal, it is
Fringecups
Tellima grandiflora

If the tiny petals are divided like feathers; plant always near water, it is
Miterwort
Mitella ovalis

greenish white
apr-may

mar-may

apr-jun

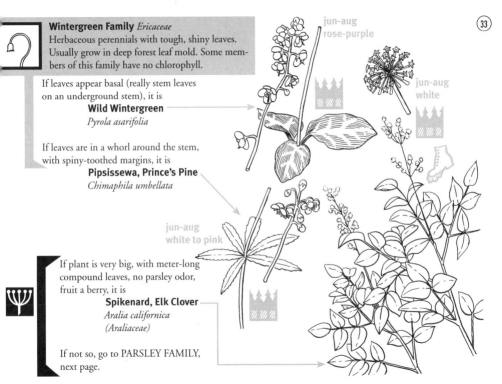

Wintergreen Family *Ericaceae*
Herbaceous perennials with tough, shiny leaves.
Usually grow in deep forest leaf mold. Some mem-
bers of this family have no chlorophyll.

jun-aug
rose-purple

jun-aug
white

If leaves appear basal (really stem leaves
on an underground stem), it is
   Wild Wintergreen
   Pyrola asarifolia

If leaves are in a whorl around the stem,
with spiny-toothed margins, it is
   Pipsissewa, Prince's Pine
   Chimaphila umbellata

jun-aug
white to pink

If plant is very big, with meter-long
compound leaves, no parsley odor,
fruit a berry, it is
   Spikenard, Elk Clover
   Aralia californica
   (Araliaceae)

If not so, go to PARSLEY FAMILY,
next page.

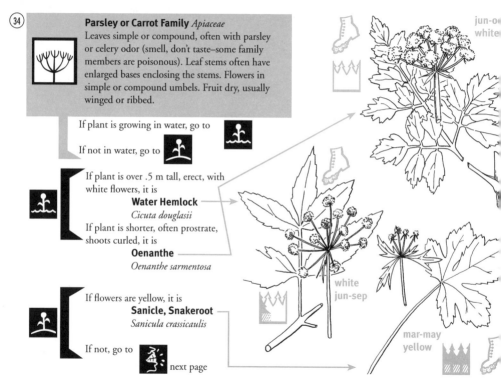

(34)

Parsley or Carrot Family *Apiaceae*
Leaves simple or compound, often with parsley
or celery odor (smell, don't taste–some family
members are poisonous). Leaf stems often have
enlarged bases enclosing the stems. Flowers in
simple or compound umbels. Fruit dry, usually
winged or ribbed.

If plant is growing in water, go to

If not in water, go to

If plant is over .5 m tall, erect, with
white flowers, it is
Water Hemlock
Cicuta douglasii

If plant is shorter, often prostrate,
shoots curled, it is
Oenanthe
Oenanthe sarmentosa

If flowers are yellow, it is
Sanicle, Snakeroot
Sanicula crassicaulis

If not, go to next page

jun-oct
white

white
jun-sep

mar-may
yellow

If plant is under 1 m tall, go to

If plant is taller, go to next page

If leaflets are fernlike, lacy, go to

If not, it is

Angelica
Angelica tomentosa

white
may-aug

If flowers are slightly enlarged at edges of flat umbels (which become cup-shaped with age) it is **Queen Anne's Lace, Wild Carrot**
Daucus carota

If flowers at edges of umbels are same size; umbels not cup-shaped; stems purple-spotted, it is **Poison Hemlock**
Conium maculatum
(illus. next page)

white
may-sep

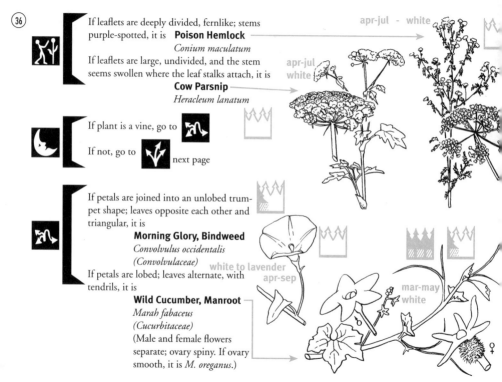

(36)

If leaflets are deeply divided, fernlike; stems purple-spotted, it is **Poison Hemlock**
Conium maculatum

If leaflets are large, undivided, and the stem seems swollen where the leaf stalks attach, it is
Cow Parsnip
Heracleum lanatum

apr-jul - white

apr-jul white

If plant is a vine, go to

If not, go to next page

If petals are joined into an unlobed trumpet shape; leaves opposite each other and triangular, it is
Morning Glory, Bindweed
Convolvulus occidentalis
(Convolvulaceae)

white to lavender
apr-sep

If petals are lobed; leaves alternate, with tendrils, it is
Wild Cucumber, Manroot
Marah fabaceus
(Cucurbitaceae)
(Male and female flowers separate; ovary spiny. If ovary smooth, it is *M. oreganus*.)

mar-may
white

If flowers are in a one-sided coil, go to
(Flowers open first at bottom of coil,
last at tip. When all are open, coil may
have straightened out. Look for a plant
with some unopened flowers.)

If not in a one-sided coil, go to page 39

If leaves are toothed or lobed, go to
WATERLEAF FAMILY, next page.

If leaf margins are entire, it is

Borage Family *Boraginaceae*
The four-lobed ovary can be seen at the base
of the style. Five stamens. These two species
each have the throat of the flower tube closed
by a ring of white scales.

If leaves are mostly pointed, long-stemmed,
basal, with some stem leaves, it is
Hound's Tongue
Cynoglossum grande
(Flowers blue-purple to pink,
sometimes both colors on
one flower.)

If all leaves are stem leaves, it is
Forget-Me-Not
Myosotis latifolia

blue, pink, white
feb-jul

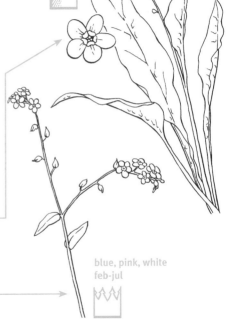

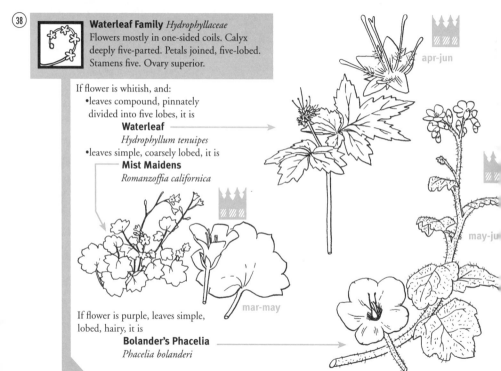

(38)

Waterleaf Family *Hydrophyllaceae*
Flowers mostly in one-sided coils. Calyx
deeply five-parted. Petals joined, five-lobed.
Stamens five. Ovary superior.

If flower is whitish, and:
• leaves compound, pinnately
  divided into five lobes, it is
       Waterleaf
       Hydrophyllum tenuipes
• leaves simple, coarsely lobed, it is
     Mist Maidens
     Romanzoffia californica

If flower is purple, leaves simple,
lobed, hairy, it is
       Bolander's Phacelia
       Phacelia bolanderi

apr-jun

may-ju

mar-may

If flower has one or two-parted style, go to 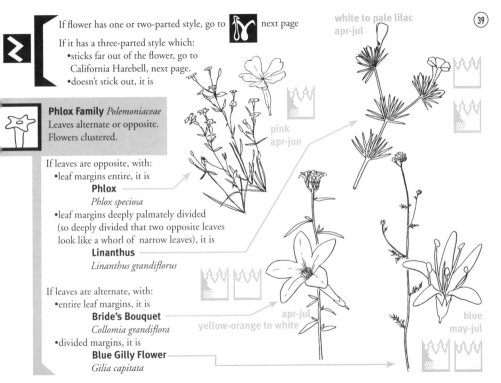 next page

If it has a three-parted style which:
- •sticks far out of the flower, go to California Harebell, next page.
- •doesn't stick out, it is

Phlox Family *Polemoniaceae*
Leaves alternate or opposite.
Flowers clustered.

If leaves are opposite, with:
- •leaf margins entire, it is
  Phlox
  Phlox speciosa
- •leaf margins deeply palmately divided
  (so deeply divided that two opposite leaves
  look like a whorl of narrow leaves), it is
  Linanthus
  Linanthus grandiflorus

If leaves are alternate, with:
- •entire leaf margins, it is
  Bride's Bouquet
  Collomia grandiflora
- •divided margins, it is
  Blue Gilly Flower
  Gilia capitata

white to pale lilac
apr-jul

pink
apr-jun

apr-jul

yellow-orange to white

blue
may-jul

40

 If leaves are opposite, whorled or basal, go to

next page

 Nightshade Family *Solanaceae*
Flowers five-lobed, folded like a fan in the bud. Five stamens, superior ovary, one stigma.

If plant is taller than .5 m, with coarse foliage, it is

Jimson Weed
Datura stramonium

If plant is shorter, with slightly lobed leaves, it is

Nightshade
Solanum americanum

summer
white

apr-nov
white to lavender

jun-sep
blue

California Harebell
Campanula prenanthoides
(Campanulaceae) (from page 39)

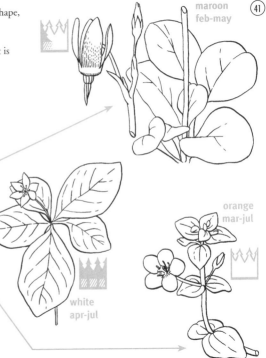

maroon
feb-may

If petals are grown together into a funnel shape, go to GENTIAN FAMILY, next page.

If they're just barely joined at their bases, it is

Primrose Family *Primulaceae*
Leaves simple. Flowers deeply lobed or parted. Stamens same number as flower lobes.

If leaves are all basal; flower hanging, with petals turned back, it is
Shooting Star
Dodecatheon hendersonii

If leaves are in a whorl under one (or few) star-like flowers, it is
Star Flower
Trientalis latifolia

If leaves are opposite, along a trailing stem, it is
Scarlet Pimpernel
Anagallis arvensis

orange
mar-jul

white
apr-jul

(42)

Gentian Family *Gentianaceae*
Plants have colorless, bitter juice. Leaves usually simple, opposite. Flowers stay on plant after withering.

may-aug

If flowers are pink, it is	**Pink Gentian**
	Centaurium davyi
If flowers are blue, it is	**Blue Gentian, Oregon Gentian**
	Gentiana affinis

Sunflower Family *Asteraceae*
A very large family, with flowers borne on heads (see diagram). Pappus takes the place of sepals. Each ovary bears one seed.

jun-

If disk and ray flowers are both present, go to page 45

If ray flowers only, go to next page

If disk flowers only, go to next page

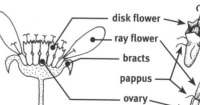

disk flower
ray flower
bracts
pappus
ovary

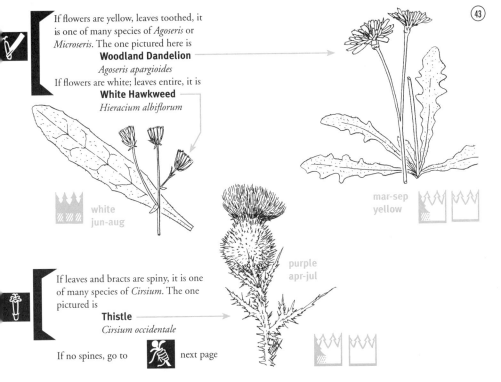

If flowers are yellow, leaves toothed, it is one of many species of *Agoseris* or *Microseris*. The one pictured here is

Woodland Dandelion
Agoseris apargioides

If flowers are white; leaves entire, it is

White Hawkweed
Hieracium albiflorum

white
jun-aug

mar-sep
yellow

purple
apr-jul

If leaves and bracts are spiny, it is one of many species of *Cirsium*. The one pictured is

Thistle
Cirsium occidentale

If no spines, go to next page

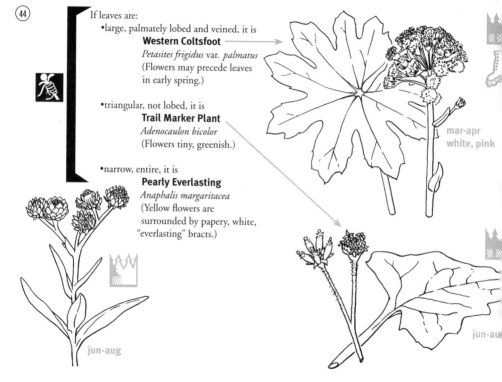

If leaves are:
- large, palmately lobed and veined, it is
  Western Coltsfoot
  Petasites frigidus var. *palmatus*
  (Flowers may precede leaves
  in early spring.)

- triangular, not lobed, it is
  Trail Marker Plant
  Adenocaulon bicolor
  (Flowers tiny, greenish.)

- narrow, entire, it is
  Pearly Everlasting
  Anaphalis margaritacea
  (Yellow flowers are
  surrounded by papery, white,
  "everlasting" bracts.)

mar-apr
white, pink

jun-aug

jun-au

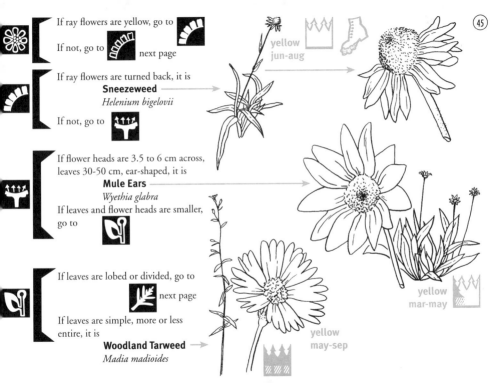

If ray flowers are yellow, go to

If not, go to next page

If ray flowers are turned back, it is
Sneezeweed
Helenium bigelovii

If not, go to

yellow
jun-aug

If flower heads are 3.5 to 6 cm across,
leaves 30-50 cm, ear-shaped, it is
Mule Ears
Wyethia glabra
If leaves and flower heads are smaller,
go to

yellow
mar-may

If leaves are lobed or divided, go to
next page

If leaves are simple, more or less
entire, it is
Woodland Tarweed
Madia madioides

yellow
may-sep

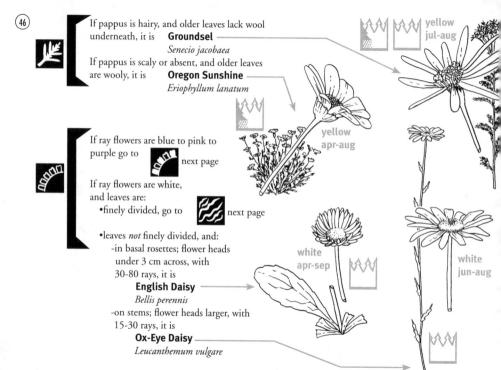

(46)

If pappus is hairy, and older leaves lack wool underneath, it is **Groundsel**
Senecio jacobaea

If pappus is scaly or absent, and older leaves are wooly, it is **Oregon Sunshine**
Eriophyllum lanatum

If ray flowers are blue to pink to purple go to next page

If ray flowers are white, and leaves are:
- finely divided, go to next page

- leaves *not* finely divided, and:
  - in basal rosettes; flower heads under 3 cm across, with 30-80 rays, it is
    English Daisy
    Bellis perennis
  - on stems; flower heads larger, with 15-30 rays, it is
    Ox-Eye Daisy
    Leucanthemum vulgare

yellow jul-aug

yellow apr-aug

white apr-sep

white jun-aug

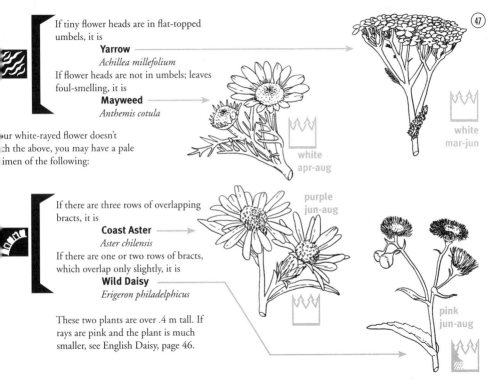

If tiny flower heads are in flat-topped umbels, it is

Yarrow
Achillea millefolium

If flower heads are not in umbels; leaves foul-smelling, it is

Mayweed
Anthemis cotula

ur white-rayed flower doesn't
:h the above, you may have a pale
imen of the following:

white
mar-jun

white
apr-aug

purple
jun-aug

If there are three rows of overlapping bracts, it is

Coast Aster
Aster chilensis

If there are one or two rows of bracts, which overlap only slightly, it is

Wild Daisy
Erigeron philadelphicus

These two plants are over .4 m tall. If rays are pink and the plant is much smaller, see English Daisy, page 46.

pink
jun-aug

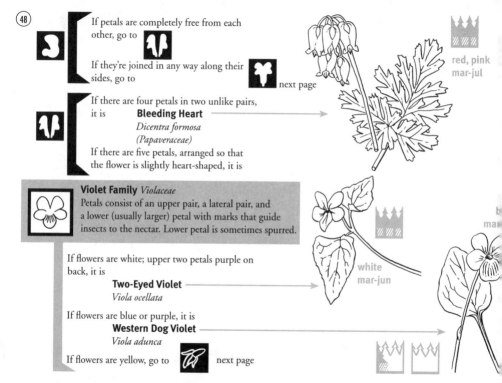

If petals are completely free from each other, go to

If they're joined in any way along their sides, go to

next page

red, pink
mar-jul

If there are four petals in two unlike pairs, it is
Bleeding Heart
Dicentra formosa
(Papaveraceae)

If there are five petals, arranged so that the flower is slightly heart-shaped, it is

Violet Family *Violaceae*
Petals consist of an upper pair, a lateral pair, and a lower (usually larger) petal with marks that guide insects to the nectar. Lower petal is sometimes spurred.

white
mar-jun

If flowers are white; upper two petals purple on back, it is
Two-Eyed Violet
Viola ocellata

If flowers are blue or purple, it is
Western Dog Violet
Viola adunca

If flowers are yellow, go to next page

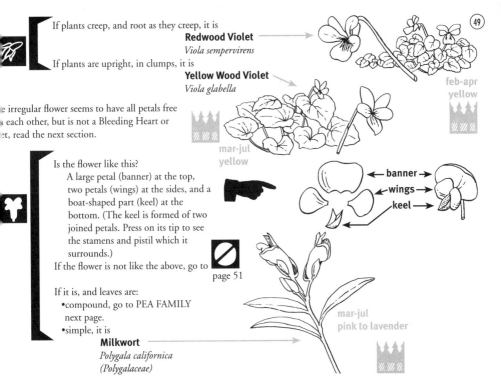

If plants creep, and root as they creep, it is
Redwood Violet
Viola sempervirens

feb-apr
yellow

If plants are upright, in clumps, it is
Yellow Wood Violet
Viola glabella

mar-jul
yellow

e irregular flower seems to have all petals free
each other, but is not a Bleeding Heart or
t, read the next section.

Is the flower like this?
A large petal (banner) at the top,
two petals (wings) at the sides, and a
boat-shaped part (keel) at the
bottom. (The keel is formed of two
joined petals. Press on its tip to see
the stamens and pistil which it
surrounds.)

←— **banner** —→
←— **wings** —→
←— **keel**

If the flower is not like the above, go to

page 51

If it is, and leaves are:
•compound, go to PEA FAMILY
next page.
•simple, it is
Milkwort
Polygala californica
(Polygalaceae)

mar-jul
pink to lavender

(50)

Pea or Bean Family *Fabaceae*
Pea-like flower with banner, wings, keel.
Compound leaves with stipules. Often ten
stamens. One pistil. Seeds in pods.

If leaves are pinnately compound, or in
threes, go to

If leaves are palmately compound, it is a
lupine. Many species inhabit the area; color
may be blue, reddish, white or yellow. A
common one, with blue flowers, is
Sky Lupine
Lupinus nanus

If there are tendrils, go to

If not, go to next page

If wing petals are partly attached to the keel, it's a
vetch. A typical one is
Vetch
Vicia americana
If wing petals are not attached to the keel,
it is a sweet pea. Typical are:
Wild Sweet Pea
Lathyrus vestitus

apr-may

apr-jun
purple, blue

**may-sep
red-purple to white**

apr-jun
white to purple,
aging yellow

Introduced Sweet
Lathyrus latifolius

If plant is self-supporting, and:
- •flowers are whitish; leaves aromatic, it is
  California Tea
  Rupertia physodes
- •flowers are yellow, in racemes; and there are large, leaf-like stipules, it is
  False Lupine
  Thermopsis macrophylla

If the plant is prostrate; flowers in umbels, it is
  Bird's Foot Trefoil
  Lotus formosissimus

If flower is reddish-brown tube, bent into a pipe shape, go to BIRTHWORT FAMILY, page 21.

If not as above, and the plant has *all* of these features:
- -square stems,
- -opposite or whorled leaves,
- -aromatic leaves,

go to MINT FAMILY, next page.

If the plant lacks one or more of these features, go to page 53

apr-jun
white

apr-jun
yellow

yellow and rose
mar-jul

Mint Family *Lamiaceae*
Aromatic plants with mostly two-lipped
flowers. Opposite or whorled leaves,
square stems. Stamens four, two short
and two long, attached to the flower
tube. Single style with a four-parted
ovary at base. Ovary grows into four
nutlets in fruit.

If flower is definitely two-lipped, go to

If flower is almost regular, not
definitely two-lipped, go to   next page

If flowers are purple with lower lips which are:
•fringed; plant .1-.5 m tall, it is
      Self Heal
      Prunella vulgaris
•flat; plant .4-.8 m tall, it is
      Wood Mint
      Stachys bullata
•concave; plant .6-1 m tall, it is
      Chamisso's Hedge Nettle
      Stachys chamissonis

If flowers are white; plant forms a long trailing
vine, it is **Yerba Buena**
      Satureja douglasii

summer

jun-oct

apr-sep

apr-sep

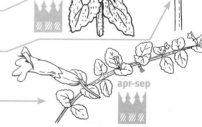

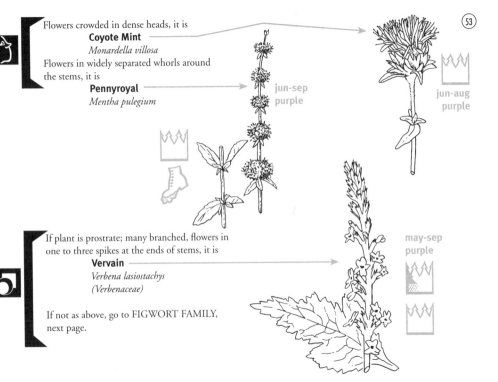

(53)

Flowers crowded in dense heads, it is
Coyote Mint
Monardella villosa
Flowers in widely separated whorls around
the stems, it is
Pennyroyal
Mentha pulegium

jun-sep
purple

jun-aug
purple

If plant is prostrate; many branched, flowers in
one to three spikes at the ends of stems, it is
Vervain
Verbena lasiostachys
(Verbenaceae)

may-sep
purple

If not as above, go to FIGWORT FAMILY,
next page.

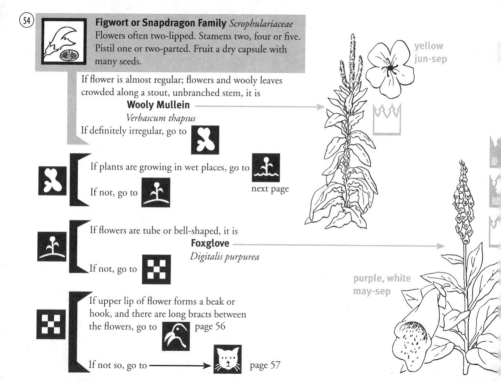

(54)

Figwort or Snapdragon Family *Scrophulariaceae*
Flowers often two-lipped. Stamens two, four or five.
Pistil one or two-parted. Fruit a dry capsule with
many seeds.

If flower is almost regular; flowers and wooly leaves
crowded along a stout, unbranched stem, it is
Wooly Mullein
Verbascum thapsus
If definitely irregular, go to

If plants are growing in wet places, go to

next page

If not, go to

If flowers are tube or bell-shaped, it is
Foxglove
Digitalis purpurea

If not, go to

If upper lip of flower forms a beak or
hook, and there are long bracts between
the flowers, go to page 56

If not so, go to page 57

yellow
jun-sep

purple, white
may-sep

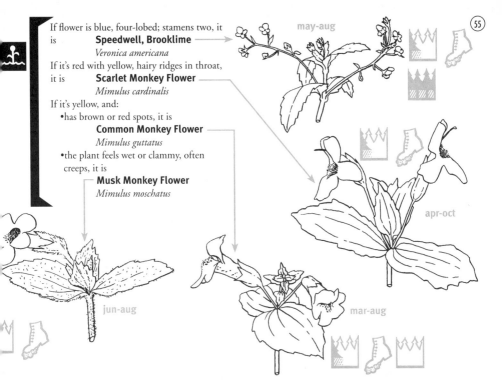

If flower is blue, four-lobed; stamens two, it is **Speedwell, Brooklime**
Veronica americana

If it's red with yellow, hairy ridges in throat, it is **Scarlet Monkey Flower**
Mimulus cardinalis

If it's yellow, and:
•has brown or red spots, it is **Common Monkey Flower**
Mimulus guttatus
•the plant feels wet or clammy, often creeps, it is

Musk Monkey Flower
Mimulus moschatus

may-aug

apr-oct

jun-aug

mar-aug

If bracts around or between flowers are green, leaflike, rather than brightly colored, it is

Parentucellia
Parentucellia viscosa

If bracts around and between the flowers are colored, rather than green, and:

•flowers are red or orange, and:

-leaf is fernlike, it is

Indian Warrior
Pedicularis densiflora

-leaf is simple, few-lobed, it is

Paintbrush
Castilleja affinis

•and flowers are white, purple or yellow, with little spots that make them resemble owl faces, it is **Owl's Clover**
Castilleja exserta

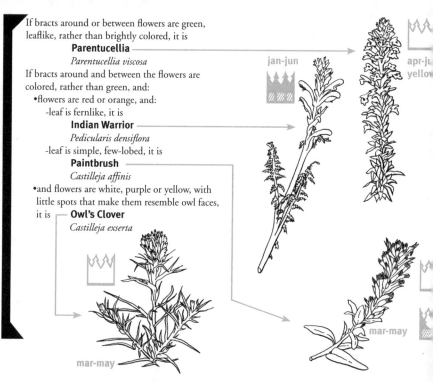

jan-jun

apr-ju
yellow

mar-may

mar-may

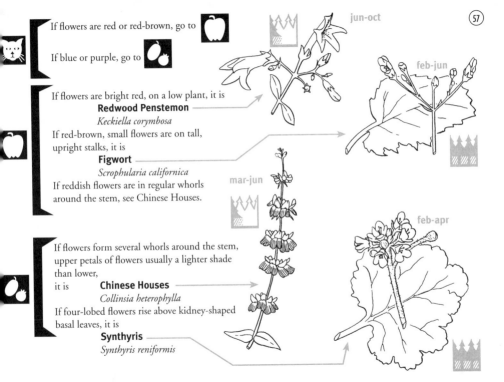

If flowers are red or red-brown, go to

If blue or purple, go to

If flowers are bright red, on a low plant, it is
Redwood Penstemon
Keckiella corymbosa
If red-brown, small flowers are on tall,
upright stalks, it is
Figwort
Scrophularia californica
If reddish flowers are in regular whorls
around the stem, see Chinese Houses.

If flowers form several whorls around the stem,
upper petals of flowers usually a lighter shade
than lower,
it is **Chinese Houses**
Collinsia heterophylla
If four-lobed flowers rise above kidney-shaped
basal leaves, it is
Synthyris
Synthyris reniformis

jun-oct

feb-jun

mar-jun

feb-apr

Achillea millefolium 47
Achlys triphylla 20
Actaea rubra 18
Adenocaulon bicolor 44
Agoseris apargioides 43
Allium unifolium 5
Allotropa virgata 2
Alum Root 31
Anagallis arvensis 41
Anaphalis margaritacea 44
Anemone oregana 18
Angelica tomentosa 35
Anthemis cotula 47
Aquilegia formosa 17
Aralia californica 33
Aristolochia californica 21
Asarum caudatum 21
Aster chilensis 47
Baneberry 18
Bear Grass 10
Bellis perennis 46
Bird's Foot Trefoil 51
Bleeding Heart 48
Blue Dicks 6
Blue-eyed Grass 7
Blue Gilly Flower 39
Bolander's Phacelia 38
Boschniakia 2
Boykinia occidentalis 30
Brassica rapa 22
Bride's Bouquet 39
Bunchberry 22
Buttercup 17, 18
California Fuchsia 24
California Harebell 40

California Lady-Slipper 4
California Pitcher Plant 26
California Poppy 19
California Tea 51
Calochortus spp. 9
Calypso bulbosa 4
Camassia quamash 11
Campanula prenanthoides 40
Cardamine spp. 23
Castilleja spp. 56
Centaurium davyi 42
Cephalanthera austiniae 3
Chamisso's Hedge Stette 52
Chickweed 28
Chimaphila umbellata 33
Chinese Houses 57
Chlorogalum pomeridianum 10
Cicuta douglasii 34
Cirsium occidentale 43
Clarkia spp. 24
Claytonia spp. 29
Clematis ligusticifolia 17
Clintonia andrewsiana 11
Collinsia heterophylla 57
Collomia grandiflora 39
Columbine 17
Conium maculatum 35, 36
Convolvulus occidentalis 36
Coral Root 3
Corallorhiza maculata 3
Cornus canadensis 22
Cow Parsnip 36
Cynoglossum grande 37
Cypripedium californicum 4
Daisy 46, 47

Darlingtonia californica 26
Datura stramonium 40
Daucus carota 35
Delphinium nudicaule 17
Dicentra formosa 48
Dichelostemma spp. 6
Digitalis purpurea 54
Disporum hookeri 14
Dodecatheon hendersonii 41
Drosera rotundifolia 26
Epilobium spp. 24
Epipactis gigantea 4
Erigeron philadelphicus 47
Eriophyllum lanatum 46
Erodium spp. 27
Erysimum capitatum 22
Erythronium californicum 10
Eschscholzia californica 19
Fairy Bells 14
Fairy Lanterns 9
False Lily-of-the-Valley 14
False Pink Asparagus 2
False Solomon's Seal 15
Farewell to Spring 24
Figwort 54-57
Firecracker Flower 6
Fireweed 24
Flax 26
Fetid Adder's Tongue 8
Forget-Me-Not 37
Foxglove 54
Fragaria vesca 16
Fringecups 32
Fritillaria spp. 12, 13
Gentian 42

Gentiana affinis 42
Geranium 27
Gilia capitata 39
Ground Cone 2
Groundsel 46
Helenium bigelovii 45
Hemitomes congestum 2
Heracleum lanatum 36
Heuchera micrantha 31
Hieracium albiflorum 44
Hound's Tongue 37
Hydrophyllum tenuipes 38
Hypericum perforatum 19
Indian Pipe 2
Indian Warrior 56
Iris 7
Ithuriel's Spear 6
Jimson Weed 40
Keckiella corymbosa 57
Klamath Weed 19
Larkspur 17
Lathyrus spp. 50
Leucanthemum vulgare 46
Lilium spp. 11-13
Lily 5-6, 8-15
Linanthus grandiflorus 39
Linum usitatissimum 26
Lithophragma affine 32
Lotus formosissimus 51
Lupine 50, 51
Lysichiton americanum 19
Madia madioides 45
Maianthemum dilatatum 14
Mallow 16
Malva neglecta 16

1 spp. 36
osa Tulip 9
eed 47
ha pulegium 53
naids 23
ort 49
lus spp. 55
's Lettuce 29
52, 53
Maidens 38
a ovalis 32
wort 32
rdella villosa 53
key Flower 55
otropa uniflora 2
ing Glory 36
 Ears 45
ard 22
sotis latifolia 37
shade 40
ar luteum ssp.
 olysepalum 15
anthe sarmentosa 34
 Leaf Onion 5
w 6
id 3-5
on Sunshine 46
s Clover 56
is oregana 25
tbrush 56
ntucellia viscosa 56
50
ly Everlasting 44
cularis densiflora 56
nyroyal 53

Petasites frigidus var.
    palmatus 44
Phacelia bolanderi 38
Phlox 39
Piggyback Plant 30
Pink 28
Piperia elegans 5
Pipevine 21
Pipsissewa 33
Poison Hemlock 35, 36
Polygala californica 49
Potentilla glandulosa 16
Prunella vulgaris 52
Pussy Ears 9
Pyrola asarifolia 33
Queen Anne's Lace 35
Ranunculus californicus 18
Raphanus sativus 23
Red Ribbons 24
Redwood Ivy 20
Redwood Sorrel 25
Romanzoffia californica 38
*Rorippa nasturtium-
    aquaticum* 23
Rupertia physodes 51
Sanicle 34
Sanicula crassicaulis 34
Satureja douglasii 52
Saxifrage 30
Scarlet Fritillary 13
Scarlet Pimpernel 41
Scoliopus bigelovii 8
Scrophularia californica 57
Self Heal 52
Senecio jacobaea 46

Shooting Star 41
Siberian Candyflower 29
Silene spp. 28
Sisyrinchium bellum 7
Skunk Cabbage 19
Smilacina spp. 15
Sneezeweed 45
Soap Plant 10
Solanum americanum 40
Speedwell 55
Spikenard 33
Spiranthes romanzoffiana 5
Stachys spp. 52
Star Flower 41
Stellaria media 28
Storksbill 27
Stream Orchis 4
Sugar Scoops 31
Sugar Stick 2
Sundew 26
Synthyris reniformis 57
Tellima grandiflora 32
Thermopsis macrophylla 51
Thistle 43
Tiarella unifoliata 31
Tolmiea menziesii 30
Trail Marker Plant 44
Trientalis latifolia 41
Trillium spp. 8
Triteleia laxa 6
Vancouveria spp. 20
Vanilla Leaf 20
Veratrum fimbriatum 14
Verbascum thapsus 54
Verbena lasiostachys 53

Veronica americana 55
Vervain 53
Vetch 50
Vicia americana 50
Viola spp. 48, 49
Violet 48, 49
Wake Robin 8
Wallflower 22
Water Cress 23
Water Hemlock 34
Waterleaf 38
Western Bittercress 23
Western Coltsfoot 44
Whipplea modesta 30
White Hawkweed 43
Wild Cucumber 36
Wild Ginger 21
Wild Radish 23
Windflower 18
Wintergreen 33
Woodland Dandelion 43
Woodland Star 32
Woodland Strawberry 16
Woodland Tarweed 45
Wooly Mullein 54
Wyethia glabra 45
Xerophyllum tenax 10
Yarrow 47
Yellow Pond Lily 15
Yerba Buena 52
Yerba de Selva 30
Zigadenus fremontii 10

Other books in the pocket-sized Finder series:

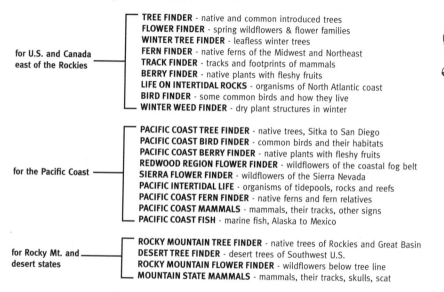

for U.S. and Canada east of the Rockies

- **TREE FINDER** - native and common introduced trees
- **FLOWER FINDER** - spring wildflowers & flower families
- **WINTER TREE FINDER** - leafless winter trees
- **FERN FINDER** - native ferns of the Midwest and Northeast
- **TRACK FINDER** - tracks and footprints of mammals
- **BERRY FINDER** - native plants with fleshy fruits
- **LIFE ON INTERTIDAL ROCKS** - organisms of North Atlantic coast
- **BIRD FINDER** - some common birds and how they live
- **WINTER WEED FINDER** - dry plant structures in winter

for the Pacific Coast

- **PACIFIC COAST TREE FINDER** - native trees, Sitka to San Diego
- **PACIFIC COAST BIRD FINDER** - common birds and their habitats
- **PACIFIC COAST BERRY FINDER** - native plants with fleshy fruits
- **REDWOOD REGION FLOWER FINDER** - wildflowers of the coastal fog belt
- **SIERRA FLOWER FINDER** - wildflowers of the Sierra Nevada
- **PACIFIC INTERTIDAL LIFE** - organisms of tidepools, rocks and reefs
- **PACIFIC COAST FERN FINDER** - native ferns and fern relatives
- **PACIFIC COAST MAMMALS** - mammals, their tracks, other signs
- **PACIFIC COAST FISH** - marine fish, Alaska to Mexico

for Rocky Mt. and desert states

- **ROCKY MOUNTAIN TREE FINDER** - native trees of Rockies and Great Basin
- **DESERT TREE FINDER** - desert trees of Southwest U.S.
- **ROCKY MOUNTAIN FLOWER FINDER** - wildflowers below tree line
- **MOUNTAIN STATE MAMMALS** - mammals, their tracks, skulls, scat

NATURE STUDY GUILD PUBLISHERS, P.O. Box 10489, Rochester, NY 1461

www.naturestudy.com • 1-800-954-2984